Praying the Scriptures

Bible-based prayers for your times of need

by
Stephanie Hoyt

Dedicated to

Grandma, who taught me to pray

and

Jeremy, Paul, and Lizzie,
who take up most of my prayer time

Table of Contents

Why should we pray the scriptures?

The Word of God is, well, the very words of God. The Bible is God speaking to us. He is using His word to teach us about himself and about how we are to relate to Him. Praying His words back to him helps us to gain His perspective in our times of need. Praying His words also shows us more of who God is.

Beyond that, sometimes we simply just don't know what to say in our prayers. We are at a loss for words, or maybe we just don't know how to pray. The Bible is our guide to prayer. We can plumb its depths and find just the right words for any and every situation we face.

How do we pray the scriptures?

There are two basic techniques for praying the Scriptures. One is to use prayers already in the Bible, but by substituting someone's name for the pronouns used in the verse. Many of these prayers can be found in the Psalms and, often, in the writings of Paul, but they are found throughout the Bible. Two, we can create prayers out of Scripture. Both techniques are used in the following prayers.

For the sake of this book, all prayers are written in italics. Sometimes you will see a Bible verse, then an italicized prayer. Other times, the Bible verse itself is in italics, denoting that the verse itself is the prayer.

My prayer is that, as you read and pray through this book, you will grow closer to God, and come to a better understanding who He is and how much He cares for you.

God bless you.

Prayers for Your Son

We have the responsibility of raising our sons to be kind, loving, Godly people, but, without prayer, we are falling short as parents. I would encourage you to make a habit of covering your son(s) in prayer every day. Even your adult children. Of course, the most obvious prayers will be for their immediate needs, such as dealing with difficult school situations, a bout with anxiety, or an important decision. But, some of the best praying we can do is pray the Scriptures over our children.

Isaiah 41:10 NLT– Don't be afraid, for I am with you. Don't be discouraged, for I am your God. I will strengthen you and help you. I will hold you up with my victorious right hand.
Thank you, Lord, that we can rest and trust in your strength. Thank you for never leaving my son, no matter where he goes or who he is with. May your strength and righteousness be real and evident to my son.

John 10:9 ESV – If anyone enters by me, he will be saved and will go in and out and find pasture.
I pray for my son's salvation, Lord. May he enter, by you, the door. I pray he finds your restful pasture. Open his eyes to see you.

Psalm 51:10-12 NIV – *Create in (my son) a pure heart, O God, and renew a steadfast spirit within (him). Do not cast (him) from your presence or take your Holy Spirit from (him). Restore to (him) the joy of your salvation and grant (him) a willing spirit, to sustain (him).*

John 10:4 ESV – When he has brought out all his own, he goes ahead of them, and the sheep follow him, for they know his voice

Thank you, Lord, for being the loving shepherd you are. Thank you for going before my son on his journey through life. I pray that you would open his ears to hear you and give him discernment to hear your voice over all the worldly voices coming at him.

Jeremiah 29:11 NLT – "For I know the plans I have for you," says the Lord, "They are plans for good and not for disaster, to give you a future and a hope."

Lord, I pray you will make your plans clear to my son. I pray that he would rest in the promise that you will give him hope and a future.

Psalm 119:36-37 NIV – *Turn (his) heart toward your statutes and not toward selfish gain. Turn (his) eyes away from worthless things; preserve (his) life according to your word.*

Romans 15:13 NIV – *May (you) the God of hope fill (my son) with all joy and peace as (he) trusts in (you), so that (he) may overflow with hope by the power of the Holy Spirit.*

Psalm 4:1 NLT – *Answer (him) when (he) calls to you, O God who declares (him) innocent. Free (him) from (his) troubles. Have mercy on (him) and hear (his) prayer.*

Proverbs 14:29 ESV – Whoever is slow to anger has great understanding, but he who has a hasty temper exalts folly. *I pray, Lord, that you would grant my son patience and understanding. Save him from his quick-tempered nature.*

Ephesians 3:14-21 NIV – *For this reason, I kneel before (you) Father, from whom (your) whole family in heaven and on earth derives its name. I pray that out of (your) glorious riches (you) may strengthen (my son) with power through your Spirit in (my son's) inner being, so that (you, Lord) may dwell in (my son's) heart through faith. And I pray that (my son), being rooted and established in love, may have power, together with all the saints, to grasp how wide and long and high and deep is (your) love, (Lord). And (for my son) to know this love that surpasses knowledge – that (my son) may be filled to the measure of all the fullness of (you) God. Now to (you, Father) who is able to do immeasurably more than all we ask or imagine, according to (your) power that is at work within us, to (you) be glory in the church and in Christ Jesus throughout all generations, for ever and ever! Amen.*

Prayers for Your Daughter

Praying for our daughters should not be the last resort, but rather our first instinct. As parents, we should pray for our daughters daily in order to cover them with prayer as they go out into the world and head (oh so fast) into their futures. The best way to do this is to have a handy list of Bible verses to pray over your daughter.

Our daughters are growing up in a volatile world with so many worldly ideas, world views, and temptations vying for their attention. Let's be diligent to guide our daughters toward Jesus through our words and actions... always covering them in prayer.

Psalm 25:4-5 NIV– *Show (her) your ways, Lord, teach (her) your paths. Guide (her) in your truth and teach (her), for you are God (her) Savior; and... my hope is in you all day long.*

Psalm 119:73 ESV – *Your hands have made and fashioned (her); give (her) understanding that (she) may learn your commandments.*

Psalm 119:36-37 NLT – *Give (her) an eagerness for your laws rather than a love of money! Turn (her) eyes from worthless things, and give (her) life through your word.*

Psalm 4:1 NIV – *Answer (her) when (she) calls to you, my righteous God. Give (her) relief from (her) distress; have mercy on (her) and hear (her) prayer.*

Psalm 5:11 NIV – But let (her) take refuge in you (and) be glad; let (her) ever sing for joy. Spread your protection over (her), that (she) who loves your name may rejoice in you.

Romans 15:13 ESV – May (you) the God of hope fill (her) with all joy and peace in believing, so that by the power of the Holy Spirit (she) may abound in hope.

Ephesians 3:16-19 NIV– I pray that out of your glorious riches you may strengthen (her) with power through your Spirit in (her) inner being, so that you may dwell in (her) heart through faith. And I pray that (she), being rooted and established in love, may have power, together with all the saints, to grasp how wide and long and high and deep is your love, and for (her) to know this love that surpasses knowledge – that (she) may be filled to the measure of all the fullness of God.

Galatians 5:16 ESV – (May she) walk by the Spirit (so she) will not gratify the desires of the flesh.

Acts 20:24 NIV– (May she) consider (her) life worth nothing to (her); (may her) only aim (be) to finish the race and complete the task the Lord Jesus has given (her) – the task of testifying to the good news of God's grace.

Acts 3:19 NLT – (May she) repent of her sins and turn to God, so that (her) sins may be wiped away.

2 Timothy 2:22 NLT – (May she) run from anything that stimulates youthful lusts. Instead, (may she) pursue righteous living, faithfulness, love, and peace. (And may she) enjoy the companionship of those who call on the Lord with pure hearts.

1 Peter 3:3-4 NIV – (May she know that her) beauty should not come from outward adornment, such as elaborate hairstyles and the wearing of gold jewelry or fine clothes. Rather, it should be that of (her) inner self, the unfading beauty of a gentle and quiet spirit, which is of great worth in God's sight.

Ephesians 6:16 ESV – (I pray that she takes) up the shield of faith, with which (she) can extinguish all the flaming darts of the evil one.

2 Peter 1:5-8 NIV – (I pray, Lord, that you would help her) make every effort to add to (her) faith goodness; and to goodness, knowledge; and to knowledge, self-control; and to self-control, perseverance; and to perseverance, godliness; and to godliness, mutual affection; and to mutual affection, love. For if (she) possesses these qualities in increasing measure, they will keep (her) from being ineffective and unproductive in (her) knowledge of the Lord Jesus Christ.

Prayers for Your Husband

Prayer is the most powerful tool we as wives have to support our husbands. No matter where they are in their spiritual journeys, we need to make it a priority to pray for our husbands every day.

Jeremiah 29:11 ESV – "For I know the plans I have for you," declares the Lord. "Plans for welfare and not for evil, plans to give you a future and a hope."
Thank you, Lord, that you have a plan for my husband and that your plans are good. I pray that you would make the path you have for him clear. Give him eyes to see you and your will for his life.

Colossians 3:23-24 NLT – *(May he) work willingly at whatever (he does), as though (he) were working for the Lord rather than for people. (May he) remember that the Lord will give (him) an inheritance as (his) reward and that the Master (he) is serving is Christ.*

John 1:12 NIV - Yet to all who did receive him, to those who believe in his name, he gave the right to become children of God.
1 Corinthians 6:17 NIV - But whoever is united with the Lord is one with him in spirit.
Father, I pray that my husband would have a clear understanding of his identity in you-that he would be able to rest in the knowledge that he is one with you in spirit and that he is your child. Protect him from the temptation to find his identity in career success, job titles, or the praise of others.

Hebrews 12:10 ESV – For they disciplined us for a short time as it seemed best to them, but (God) disciplines us for our good, that we may share in his holiness.

Lord, I pray for my husband's sanctification. I pray you would continue to lead him towards holiness. Discipline him when need be for his own good in order that he may share in your holiness. Give him the courage, strength, and desire to pursue holiness.

Proverbs 12:1 ESV – Whoever loves discipline loves knowledge, but whoever hates reproof is stupid.

Father, I pray you would give my husband a humble and teachable spirit. I pray you would give him ears to hear your instructions and a heart to follow your teaching.

1 Corinthians 10:13 NIV - No temptation has overtaken you except what is common to mankind. And God is faithful; he will not let you be tempted beyond what you can bear, but when you are tempted, he will also provide a way out so that you can endure it.

Lord, thank you for providing a way out of temptation. Thank you that we are never tempted beyond what we can bear. Please keep my husband from temptation-whatever form it may take. May he know your strength to be able to walk away from all the temptations the world throws at him. Deliver him from evil.

Ephesians 5:23 ESV - For the husband is the head of the wife even as Christ is the head of the church, his body, and is himself its Savior.

I *pray, God, that my husband would humbly take the role of head of our household and that he would love me as Christ loves the church. I pray that you would give him wisdom as he directs our household.*

Philippians 4:8 NLT – *(May he) fix (his) thoughts on what is true, and honorable, and right, and pure, and lovely, and admirable. (That he would) think about things that are excellent and worthy of praise.*

Colossians 2:8 NLT – *Don't let anyone capture (him) with empty philosophies and high sounding nonsense that come from human thinking and from spiritual powers of this world, rather than from Christ.*

Proverbs 14:26 NIV - Whoever fears the Lord has a secure fortress, and for their children it will be a refuge.
Proverbs 20:7 NIV - The godly walk with integrity; blessed are their children who follow them.
Ephesians 6:4 NIV - Fathers, do not exasperate your children; instead, bring them up in the training and instruction of the Lord.
Lord, I pray for my husband to be the faithful, loving father you would have him be. I pray that he would be an example to our children in word and deed and that the Holy Spirit would guide him as he instructs them. I pray that he would have patience with them and not exasperate them. I pray that you would hold firm the bonds between my husband and our children throughout their lives.

James 4:7 NLT – So humble yourselves before God. Resist the devil, and he will flee from you.
Hebrews 4:15-16 NIV – For we do not have a high priest who is unable to empathize with our weaknesses, but we have one who has been tempted in every way, just as we are-yet he did not sin. Let us then approach God's throne of grace with confidence, so that we may receive mercy and find grace to help us in our time of need.
Thank you, Lord, that you can empathize with our weaknesses. I pray you will help my husband find a way out of his bad habits. I pray that he would not be mastered by them. And I pray your grace will help him in his time of need.

Prayers for the Prodigal

A child, spouse, friend... watching someone we love turn their back on their faith is a heartbreaking experience. But, God is good! Though our loved ones turn their backs on God, he does not turn his back on them! Keep loving them and praying for them.

Philippians 1:6 NLT – And I am certain that God, who began a good work within you, will continue his work until it is finally finished on the day when Christ Jesus returns.
I pray, Lord, that you who began a good work in _____, will continue this work until it is finally finished on the day Christ Jesus returns.

Ezekiel 34:16 NLT – I will search for my lost ones who strayed away, and I will bring them safely home again. I will bandage the injured and strengthen the weak.
Lord, thank you for your faithfulness to _____. I pray you will search for your lost one, _____, who strayed away and bring them safely home again.

Matthew 18:12-14 NLT – (Parable of the lost sheep) If a man has a hundred sheep and one of them wanders away, what will he do? Won't he leave the ninety-nine others on the hills and go out to search for the one who is lost? And if he finds it, I tell you the truth, he will rejoice over it more than the ninety-nine who didn't wander away! In the same way, it is not my heavenly Father's will that even one of these little ones should perish.
Oh, heavenly Father, in your loving kindness it is not your will for any of your sheep to perish. Have mercy on _____ and, as the good shepherd, I pray you will search for _____ who is lost and return them safely to the flock.

Hebrews 10:23 NLT – Let us hold tightly without wavering to the hope we affirm, for God can be trusted to keep His promise.

You have promised to search for the ones who have strayed. I praise you and thank you that I can trust in your promise to not let _____ perish!

2 Peter 3:9 NIV – The Lord is not slow in keeping his promise, as some understand slowness. Instead, he is patient with you, not wanting anyone to perish, but everyone to come to repentance.

Thank you, Lord, for both your patience with _____ and your desire for _____ not to perish. I pray you will lead _____ to repentance.

Luke 5:31-32 NIV – Jesus answered them, "It is not the healthy who need a doctor, but the sick. I have not come to call the righteous, but sinners to repentance."

Thank you Father for sending your son to call the sick. I pray _____ will recognize their sinful nature and be led to repentance.

Luke 15:24 ESV - "For this my son was dead and is alive again; he was lost , and is found." So they began to celebrate.

Oh, Lord, I pray that _____, who is lost, will be found again! Lead _____ back to you, Gracious Father. Make them alive again.

Hebrews 7:25 ESV – Consequently, he is able to save to the uttermost those who draw near to God through him, since he always lives to make intercession for them.

Thank you Holy Father for sending your son Jesus in order that through him we have a path to you. Thank you Jesus for interceding with God on _____'s behalf. Lord, I pray that _____ will find the path to Jesus that leads to you.

John 3:16 ESV – For God so loved the world, that he gave his only Son, that whoever believes in him should not perish but have eternal life.

Thank you, God, for loving us and giving us your Son for our salvation. I pray that _____ will believe in you, that they would not perish, and that they would have eternal life.

Acts 3:19 NIV – Repent, then, and turn to God, so that your sins may be wiped out, that times of refreshing may come from the Lord.

I pray that _____ will repent of their sins and turn back to you so that their sins may be wiped away and their soul refreshed.

Prayers for Your Marriage

Is your marriage in trouble? Or is it going great? Either way, we need to continue to cover our marriages in prayer. Marriage is a covenant relationship between two people and God. Prayer is one way we acknowledge God is present in our marriages.

1 Corinthians 13:4-5 NIV - Love is patient, love is kind. It does not envy, it does not boast, it is not proud. It does not dishonor others, it is not self-seeking, it is not easily angered, it keeps no records of wrongs. *You are love, God, and your love is holy. I pray my love for _____ would be patient and kind… not jealous, boastful, or proud… not demanding, irritable, or keeping records of wrongs. Humble me, Lord, to show love to _____ as you have shown love to me.*

Ephesians 4:2-3 NLT – Always be humble and gentle. Be patient with each other, making allowance for each other's faults because of your love. Make every effort to keep yourselves united in the Spirit, binding yourselves together with peace.
Lord, grant me humbleness, gentleness, and peace with _____. I pray for a spirit of grace that will allow me to make allowances for _____'s faults, as you have shown me grace for mine. Keep us united in the Spirit, and bind us together with peace.

Ecclesiastes 4:9-10 NLT – Two people are better off than one, for they can help each other succeed. If one person falls, the other can reach out and help. But someone who falls alone is in real trouble.
Thank you, Lord, for bringing _____ into my life to be my partner and helper. I pray we will have hearts that desire the best for each other and hearts that desire to help each other when we fall.

25

Mark 10:9 ESV – What therefore God has joined together, let not man separate.

Thank you, Lord, for your sovereignty in joining me and _____ together in marriage. I pray no one or nothing will tear us apart.

1 Peter 4:8 NIV - Above all, love each other deeply, because love covers a multitude of sins.

I pray you would give us a deep love for one another; the love that covers a multitude of sins.

John 15:12 NLT – This is my commandment: Love each other in the same way I have loved you.

Oh, Lord, your love abounds! Help me and _____ to love each other in the same way you love us.

2 Thessalonians 3:3 NLT - But the Lord is faithful; he will strengthen you and guard you from the evil one.

We rejoice in your faithfulness! I pray you would strengthen us and guard our marriage from the evil one who would like nothing more than to tear us apart.

Genesis 2:24 NIV - That is why a man leaves his father and mother and is united to his wife, and they become one flesh.

Thank you. Lord, for uniting me with _____. I pray you would strengthen our bond and that you would show us how to live as one flesh.

Colossians 3:13 NIV - Bear with each other and forgive one another if any of you has a grievance against someone. Forgive as the Lord forgave you.

_____ and I are both sinners who make mistakes. I pray you would help us to forgive each other for our missteps (whether committed in word or deed), as you have forgiven us.

Ephesians 4:32 ESV – Be kind to one another, tenderhearted, forgiving one another, as God in Christ forgave you.
As we journey through this fallen and broken world, I pray that _____ and I can be kind, tenderhearted, and forgiving toward one another, just as you have been toward us.

Prayers for Anxiety

" Anxiety is the greatest evil that can befall a soul, except sin. God commands you to pray but he forbids you to worry."
St. Francis de Sales

Various studies estimate that roughly 18% of adults in the US suffer from anxiety. For many Christians suffering from anxiety, counseling and medical attention may be needed. Our first line of defense, though, should always be prayer. Let's let the Scriptures be our prayer guide.

1 John 4:18 ESV - There is no fear in love. But perfect love casts out fear. For fear has to do with punishment, and whoever fears has not been perfected in love.
Father God, you are love and your love is holy and perfect. With you, there is no fear of the future. Lord, please grant me this "perfect love" that does not fear.

Psalms 46:10 ESV - Be still and know that I am God.
Father, I am weary with worry. My mind seems to never stop racing. Help me to be still, breathe, and focus on you, so I will know you are God.

Isaiah 41:10 NIV - So do not fear, for I am with you; do not be dismayed, for I am your God. I will strengthen you and help you; I will uphold you with my righteous right hand.
Thank you, Lord, for your promise to never leave me, to strengthen and help me, and to uphold me with your righteous right hand. Oh, Lord, how I pray that the truth of these promises would be real to me and that these promises would sustain me and calm me in my times of anxiety.

Joshua 1:9 NIV - Have I not commanded you? Be strong and courageous. Do not be afraid; do not be discouraged, for the Lord your God will be with you wherever you go.

You are with me wherever I go, but I don't always remember that. Oh, Father, I pray that that truth would be real to me. I pray that the Holy Spirit would constantly remind me. Guard me from discouragement and fear, and grant me strength and courage.

John 14:1 NLT - Do not let your hearts be troubled. Trust in God, and trust also in me.

It is so easy to be troubled by the things of this world… relationships, work, family, politics, illness. I pray I can guard my heart. Lord. Protect me from negative thoughts that only increase my anxiety.

2 Timothy 1:7 NLT – God has not given us a Spirit of fear and timidity, but of power, love, and self-discipline.

Lord, I confess I give in to timidity often. I fear and worry constantly. By doing so, I show a lack of faith in you and your promises. Please forgive me. I pray you would clear my mind and my heart, so that I can see and apply the spirit of power, love, and self-discipline you have given me.

Isaiah 26:3-4 NIV - You will keep in perfect peace those whose minds are steadfast, because they trust in you. Trust in the Lord forever, for the Lord, the Lord himself, is the Rock eternal.

Father God, I long for your perfect peace. Please, tear down these walls that keep me from trusting you completely. Help my mind to become steadfast and focused on you.

Psalms 94:19 ESV – When the cares of my heart are many, your consolations cheer my soul.
Help me, Lord, to remember all the ways you have consoled me in the past, so that I may sing your praises and be joyful.

Philippians 4:6-7 NIV - Do not be anxious about anything, but in every situation, by prayer and petition, with thanksgiving, present your requests to God. And the peace of God, which transcends all understanding, will guard your hearts and minds in Christ Jesus.
Thank you, Lord, that I can come to you at any time with any request. I pray that my first thought in any and every situation would be to come to you in prayer.

Psalms 34:4 NLT – I prayed to the Lord, and he answered me. He freed me from my fears.
Lord, thank you that you can and do deliver us from all our fears. Open my eyes and heart to see you, so that the mere thought of you would outshine the anxiety and fear within me.

Prayers for Hope

We can all use some hope. What are you hoping for? A million dollars? Reconciliation with a loved one? For your political party to win the next election? If so, you are putting your hope in the wrong place… the things of this world. The only true hope we have is in the promises of God.

Isaiah 40:31 NLT - But those who trust in the Lord will find new strength. They will soar high on wings like eagles. They will run and not grow weary. They will walk and not faint.
Lord, I hope for all the wrong things. I have convinced myself that if only I could have _____, I would be fine. The only true hope is in you. I pray you would help me keep my hope in you so that, one day, I will soar on wings like eagles and run and not grow faint or weary.

Romans 15:13 NIV - *May (you) the God of hope fill (me) with all joy and peace as (I) trust in (you), so that (I) may overflow with hope by the power of the Holy Spirit.*

Romans 8:28 ESV – And we know that for those who love God all things work together for good, for those who are called according to his purpose.
Thank you, Lord, that no matter what is happening all around me, no matter my circumstances, you are working everything for my good. I pray I can find my hope in this promise.

Romans 8:38-39 NIV - For I am convinced that neither death or life, neither angels nor demons, neither the present nor the future, nor any powers, neither height nor depth, nor anything else in all of creation, will be able to separate us from the love of God that is in Christ Jesus our Lord.

Lord, I pray my hope will rest in the fact that nothing can ever separate me from you and your love. May this truth sustain me.

Romans 8:18 ESV – For I consider that the sufferings of this present time are not worth comparing with the glory that is to be revealed to us. *Father, I confess that I often lose hope, because I am too focused on my own sufferings. I pray that my hope would be in the "glory that is to be revealed".*

Jeremiah 29:11 NIV - "For I know the plans I have for you," declares the Lord, "plans to prosper you and not to harm you, plans to give you hope and a future."

Thank you, Lord, for the plans you have for me. I lose hope when my own plans fail. Lead me in the way you would have me go so that I will receive the hope and the future you have for me.

Proverbs 23:18 ESV – Surely there is a future, and your hope will not be cut off.

Oh, Father, thank you for a future hope in You! Thank you, that this hope is eternal and can never be cut off.

1 Peter 1:13 ESV – Therefore, preparing your minds for action, and being sober-minded, set your hope fully on the grace that will be brought to you at the revelation of Jesus Christ.

I have placed my hope in so many things that have failed me, Lord. But, your hope never fails! I pray I can keep my mind and hope set "on the grace to be brought to (me) when Jesus Christ is revealed at his coming."

Ephesians 1:18-19a NIV - *I pray that the eyes of (my) heart may be enlightened in order that (I) may know the hope to which (you have) called (me), the riches of (your) glorious inheritance in (your) holy people, and (your) incomparably great power for us who believe.*

Prayers for Peace

Peace and calm are more and more elusive with the growing cacophony of noise attacking us from every angle. Social media, 24-hour news channels, and constant bickering inside our workplaces, our communities, and even our churches and homes, have left us anxious, weary, and in desperate need of the peace of God.

In Judges chapter 6, Gideon builds an altar and names it Yahweh-Shalom (the Lord is peace). Our peace is God and in God alone will we find the peace we crave.

Romans 5:1 ESV - Therefore, since we have been justified by faith, we have peace with God through our Lord Jesus Christ.
Thank you, Lord, that I am justified through faith and, because of that truth, I have peace with God through my Lord Jesus Christ. I pray the Spirit would constantly remind me of this justification that leads to peace, that this peace may be real and evident in me.

1 John 4:18 NIV - There is no fear in love. But perfect love drives out fear, because fear has to do with punishment. The one who fears is not made perfect in love.
Thank you, Father, that your love drives out fear and leads me to a place of peace.

John 16:33 NLT – I have told you all this so that you may have peace in me. Here on earth you will have many trials and sorrows. But take heart, because I have overcome the world.

Thank you, Father, for sending your son, Jesus Christ, to tell us all about you and the hope that you provide, so that I may have peace. Help me, Lord, to take heart because Jesus has overcome the world.

Romans 15:13 NIV - *May the God of hope fill (me) with all joy and peace as (I) trust in him, so that (I) may overflow with hope by the power of the Holy Spirit.*

John 14:27 ESV – Peace I leave with you; my peace I give you. Not as the world gives do I give to you. Let not your hearts be troubled, neither let them be afraid.
Thank you, Lord, for the peace that has been given to me through Jesus. Do not let my heart be troubled and keep me from fear.

Psalm 4:8 NIV - *In peace I will lie down and sleep, for you alone, Lord, make me dwell in safety.*

Isaiah 32:17-18 NIV - The fruit of that righteousness will be peace; its effect will be quietness and confidence forever. May people live in peaceful dwelling places, in secure homes, in undisturbed places of rest.
Lord, grant me the peace that comes from righteousness, so that I would have the effect of quietness and confidence forever. I pray to live in a peaceful dwelling place, in a secure home, and in undisturbed places of rest.

Isaiah 53:5 NIV - But he was pierced for our transgressions, he was crushed for our iniquities; the punishment that brought us peace was on him, and by his wounds we are healed.

Thank you, Lord, for suffering the punishment that should have been mine. Because of that punishment, I can have peace. I pray that peace would be real to me now.

Philippians 4:6-7 NIV - Do not be anxious about anything, but in every situation, by prayer and petition, with thanksgiving, present your requests to God. And the peace of God, which transcends all understanding, will guard your hearts and your minds in Christ Jesus.

Thank you that in every situation, by prayer and petition, with thanksgiving, I can present my requests to you. Lord, help me to let go of my anxiety. Guard my heart and mind in Christ Jesus, I pray.

2 Thessalonians 3:16 NIV - *Now may the Lord of peace himself give (me) peace at all times and in every way. The Lord be with (me).*

Prayers for Wisdom

True wisdom is from God, not from textbooks, teachers, scientists, or even from our own understanding. Our Father in heaven gives us this wisdom freely, if only we can see it. But how can we grab hold of this wisdom? Scripture tell us how.

Proverbs 9:10 NLT – The fear of the Lord is the foundation of wisdom. Knowledge of the Holy One results in good judgment.
True wisdom begins and ends with you, Father. Teach me to fear you, Lord, so I may gain wisdom. Give me the knowledge of you that leads to understanding.

Psalms 90:12 NIV - *Teach us to number our days, that we may gain a heart of wisdom.*

Proverbs 11:2 NLT – Pride leads to disgrace, but with humility comes wisdom.
Lord, keep me from having a prideful spirit, I pray. Show me humility so that I may gain wisdom.

Proverbs 13:20 ESV – Whoever walks with the wise becomes wise, but the companion of fools will suffer harm.
Thank you, Lord, for the wisdom you so freely give. I pray for friendship with wise people who know you closely and can help me become wise. Give me discernment to recognize the "fools" attempting to lead me astray.

James 1:5 ESV - If any of you lacks wisdom, let him ask God, who gives generously to all without reproach, and it will be given to him.

Thank you, Lord, for generously providing wisdom to all without finding fault. I ask, now, Lord, for your wisdom.

Ephesians 5:15-17 NIV - Be very careful, then, how you live - not as unwise but as wise, making the most of every opportunity, because the days are evil. Therefore do not be foolish, but understand what the Lord's will is.

Help me to live "not as unwise, but as wise". Help me to make "the most of every opportunity, because the days are evil." Keep me from foolishness, but help me understand what your will is.

James 3:17 ESV - But the wisdom from above is first pure, then peaceable, gentle, open to reason, full of mercy and good fruits, impartial and sincere.

Father, I pray you would grant me "the wisdom from above (that) is first pure, then peaceable, gentle, open to reason, full of mercy and good fruits, impartial and sincere."

Proverbs 13:10 ESV – By insolence comes nothing but strife, but with those who take advice is wisdom.

Lord, I pray for wise advice that leads to wisdom, and protect me from the pride that leads to strife.

1 Corinthians 3:18 ESV – Let no one deceive himself. If anyone among you thinks that he is wise in this age, let him become a fool that he may become wise.

Do not let me deceive myself, Lord. Help me to lose the standards of wisdom of this age, that I may become wise.

James 3:13-15 NIV - Who is wise and understanding among you? Let them show it by their good life, by deeds done in humility that comes from wisdom. But if you harbor bitter envy and selfish ambition in your hearts, do not boast about it or deny the truth. Such "wisdom" does not come down from heaven but is earthly, unspiritual, demonic. *Lord, I pray for the wisdom that leads to humility. Strip my heart of the earthly, unspiritual, demonic "wisdom" that leads to bitter envy and selfish ambition.*

Prayers for God's Will

One of my college Bible professors once got on to our class about constantly struggling to find God's will for our lives. What should I major in? Should I take this job or that one? He chastised us for pausing our journeys and waiting for God to send a neon sign with clear instructions. His point was that, when faced with a decision, we are to pray for God to show the way forward. Then, neon sign or not, we are to just keep moving forward. God is sovereign. He will get us to where he needs us to be.

The Bible is full of instructions on what God wants from us-His will for all of us. Focus on those, and the rest will fall into place.

Matthew 6:33 ESV – But seek first the kingdom of God and his righteousness, and all these things will be added to you.
Lord, I confess I am often guilty of focusing on "all these things" before focusing on your kingdom and righteousness. Help me, I pray, to put you first and to put my faith in your promise that then "all these things will be added to" me.

1 Thessalonians 5:16-18 ESV – Rejoice always, pray without ceasing, give thanks in all circumstances; for this is the will of God in Christ Jesus for you.
Thank you, Father, again, for this clear call of your will for my life. Help me to set my mind on prayer, thanksgiving, and rejoicing.

Colossians 4:17 ESV - See to it that you fulfill the ministry that you have received in the Lord.
Lord, open my eyes to see the ministry you have for me right here, right now. Give me strength and wisdom to complete this ministry.

Proverbs 3:5-6 ESV - Trust in the Lord with all your heart, and do not lean on your own understanding. In all your ways acknowledge him, and he will make straight your paths.

Lord, please show me all the ways in which I am not submitting to you. Help me to trust you and not rely on my own understanding. Grant me the wisdom to know the difference.

Jeremiah 29:11 ESV - For I know the plans I have for you, declares the Lord, plans for welfare and not for evil, plans to give you a future and a hope.

Thank you, Father, for having a plan for my life. Thank you for this hope and future. Get me to where you need me to be to fulfill your will.

Luke 9:23 ESV – Then he said to all, "If anyone would come after me, let him deny himself and take up his cross daily and follow me. For whoever would save his life will lose it, but whoever loses his life for my sake will save it."

As a Christian, I live my life for you, Lord. Give me the faith and courage to deny myself and follow you wherever you lead me.

Ephesians 5:15-20 NIV - Be very careful, then, how you live - not as unwise but as wise, making the most of every opportunity, because the days are evil. Therefore do not be foolish, but understand what the Lord's will is. Do not get drunk on wine, which leads to debauchery. Instead, be filled with the Spirit, speaking to one another with psalms, hymns, and songs from the Spirit. Sing and make music from your heart to the Lord, always giving thanks to God the Father for everything, in the name of our Lord Jesus Christ.

Lord, I pray I would be filled with the Spirit and that the Spirit would give me songs and hymns of praise throughout the day. Show me how to make the most of every opportunity. Grant me wisdom.

Micah 6:8 NIV - He has shown you, O mortal, what is good. And what does the Lord require of you? To act justly and to love mercy and to walk humbly with your God.

Thank you, Lord, for this clear expectation of how I am to live my life. Whatever situation I am in, wherever I may be, help me to act justly, love mercy, and walk humbly with you.

John 10 :4 ESV - When he has brought out all his own, he goes before them, and the sheep follow him, for they know his voice.

Father, thank you for leading me on this journey through life. I pray, Lord, I would recognize your voice above all the other voices vying for my attention.

Romans 12:2 NIV - Do not be conformed to the pattern of this world, but be transformed by the renewing of your mind. Then you will be able to test and approve what God's will is - his good, pleasing and perfect will.

Lord, I pray for a renewing of my mind. Help me to see where I am "conforming to the pattern of this world", so that I can break those thought habits. Help me to discern your good, pleasing, and perfect will.

Philippians 2:12-13 NIV - Therefore, my dear friends, as you have always obeyed - not only in my presence, but now much more in my absence - continue to work out your salvation with fear and trembling, for it is God who works in you to will and to act in order to fulfill his good purpose.

Lord, thank you that you are working your will in me to fulfill your good purpose. Show me how to work out my own salvation with fear and trembling.

Prayers for Political Leaders

I admit I am guilty of harshly judging and even loathing many of my political leaders. Are you the same? With so much discord in our world surrounding politics, how about we pray instead of ridicule? Let's humbly come before the Lord and lift up our leaders. God is good and he desires their salvation as much as anyone else.

Romans 13:1 NLT Everyone must submit to governing authorities. For all authority comes from God, and those in positions of authority have been placed there by God.
Lord, I often forget that those in political positions are there because of your sovereignty. For whatever reason, you have them in these positions of power. Help me, Lord, to respect them and to humbly subject myself to them.

Proverbs 11:14 NLT Without wise leadership, a nation falls; there is safety in having many advisers.
Lord, I pray for wise advisers for our leaders. Bring forth Godly men and women to help lead this land.

1 Timothy 2:1-2 NLT – I urge you first of all, to pray for all people. Ask God to help them; intercede on their behalf, and give thanks for them. Pray this way for kings and all who are in authority so that we can live peaceful and quiet lives marked by godliness and dignity.
I thank you, Lord, that in your sovereignty you have appointed our political leaders. I pray for their salvation, their understanding of you, and for wisdom for them to lead us. I pray for leaders who will lead us to peaceful and quiet lives.

Daniel 2:21 NIV - He changes times and seasons; he deposes kings and raises up others. He gives wisdom to the wise and knowledge to the discerning.
Your power is mighty, Lord. You set the times and seasons. You rule far above our earthly leaders. Give wisdom and knowledge to us all, including our leadership, Lord.

Psalms 72:1-2 NIV - *Endow the king with your justice, O God, the royal son with your righteousness. May he judge your people in righteousness, your afflicted ones with justice.*

Proverbs 29:4 NLT – A just king gives stability to his nation, but one who demands bribes destroys it.
I pray our leaders would not be greedy for bribes, but eager for the justice that gives a country stability.

Ezekiel 34:2b-4 NLT - What sorrow awaits you shepherds who feed yourselves instead of your flocks. Shouldn't shepherds feed their sheep? You drink the milk, wear the wool, and butcher the best animals, but you let your flocks starve. You have not taken care of the weak. You have not tended the sick or bound up the injured. You have not gone looking for those who have wandered away and are lost. Instead, you have ruled them with harshness and cruelty.
Lord, I pray our political leaders would not rule with harshness and cruelty. I pray they would have hearts to help the sick, the poor, the hungry, and the injured.

Isaiah 11:2 NIV - *(May) the Spirit of the Lord rest on (our leaders) - the Spirit of wisdom and understanding, the Spirit of counsel and of might, the Spirit of the knowledge of the fear of the Lord - and (may our leaders) delight in the fear of the Lord.*

Isaiah 31:1 NLT - What sorrow awaits those who look to Egypt for help, trusting their horses, chariots, and charioteers and depending on the strength of human armies instead of looking to the Lord, the Holy One of Israel.

Father, I pray our leaders would put their trust in you, not in the might of their armies.

Prayers for Revival

Our world, our nation, even - at times - our own churches, homes, and souls are starving for revival. In this parched and dry land, God longs to renew our spiritual vigor. He pours out his living water, and revives us, so that we will rejoice in him. Let's pray for revival in our land. God is good! In him, we can have spiritual fullness.

Isaiah 44:3 NLT - For I will pour out water to quench your thirst and to irrigate your parched fields. And I will pour out my Spirit on your descendants, and my blessing on your children.
Pour out your water to quench our thirst and to irrigate our parched fields. Pour out your Spirit on our descendants, and your blessing on our children, I pray.

Romans 8:29 NLT - For God knew his people in advance, and he chose them to become like his Son, so that his Son would be firstborn among many brothers and sisters.
God, you know in advance those you have chosen to become like your son. Open their eyes to see you and soften their hearts to receive you.

Psalm 85:6 NLT - *Will you not revive us again, that your people may rejoice in you?*

2 Chronicles 7:14 NIV - If my people, who are called by my name, will humble themselves and pray and seek my face and turn from their wicked ways, then I will hear from heaven, and I will forgive their sin and will heal their land.

Lord, I pray we - your followers - can humble ourselves, seek your face, and turn from our evil ways, and that you will forgive our sins and heal our land.

Acts 1:8 NLT - But you will receive power when the Holy Spirit comes upon you. And you will be my witnesses, telling people about me everywhere-in Jerusalem, throughout Judea, in Samaria, and to the ends of the earth.
Thank you, Lord, for the gift of your Holy Spirit. I pray you would lead your Spirit-filled followers to be your witness to the ends of the earth.

Psalm 22:27 NIV - *(May) all the ends of the earth remember and turn to the Lord, and all the families of the nations bow down before him.*

John 3:16 NIV - For God so loved the world that he gave his one and only Son, that whoever believes in him shall not perish but have eternal life.
In your extraordinary love, you gave your one and only Son, that whoever believes in him shall not perish but have eternal life. Lord, I pray this remarkable truth will reach in and revive the hearts of your followers. I pray this truth will soften the hearts of unbelievers, so that they will turn from their wicked ways and follow you.

Isaiah 57:15 NIV - For this is what the high and exalted One says-he who lives forever, whose name is holy: "I live in a high and holy place, but also with the one who is contrite and lowly in spirit, to revive the spirit of the lowly and to revive the heart of the contrite."

You are the high and exalted One, who lives forever and whose name is holy! Oh, Lord, I pray you would lead us to have contrite hearts. I pray, you would graciously revive the spirit of the lowly and revive the hearts of the contrite.

Psalm 80:19 NIV - *Restore us, Lord God Almighty; make your face shine on us, that we may be saved.*

2 Timothy 4:3-4 NLT For a time is coming when people will no longer listen to sound and wholesome teaching. They will follow their own desires and will look for teachers who will tell them whatever their itching ears want to hear. They will reject the truth and chase after myths.

Lord, it saddens us to see the number of people who will not put up with sound doctrine. Instead, to suit their own desires, they gather around them a great number of teachers to say what their itching ears want to hear. They have turned their ears away from your truth and, instead, follow myths. Oh, Lord, I pray you would show them the error of their ways. Soften their hearts that they may accept your truth. Expose the wickedness of these false teachers and, in your mercy, lead them to true repentance and salvation.

Prayers for Unity

Disunity and conflict are all around us these days. There seems to be polarizing discord at every turn - between ideologies, between political parties, between races, even between members of our churches and members of our families. As followers of Christ, we need to live as a city on a hill; an example of what unity is and how it can be achieved. God clearly calls us to unity and His Word shows us how to be unified with others.

Colossians 3:15 NIV - *(May) the peace of Christ rule in (our) hearts, since as members of one body (we) were called to peace. And (may we always) be thankful.*

Romans 12:16 ESV - Live in harmony with one another. Do not be haughty, but associate with the lowly. Never be wise in your own sight. (personal prayer) *I pray I can live in harmony with others. That I would not be proud, but would be willing to associate with people of low position, and that I would not be conceited.*
(communal prayer) *I pray that we can live in harmony with one another. That we would not be proud, but we would be willing to associate with people of low position, and that we would not be conceited.*

1 John 3:18 ESV – Little children, let us not love in word or talk but in deed and in truth.
Lord, I pray our love for others would be evident with our actions and in truth. I pray our words and speech would match our actions.

1 Thessalonians 5:14 ESV - And we urge you, brothers, admonish the idle, encourage the fainthearted, help the weak, be patient with them all.
As your followers striving for unity, Lord, I pray you would help us to lovingly warn those among us who are idle and disruptive. Help us, also, to encourage the disheartened, help the weak, and be patient with everyone.

Colossians 4:6 NIV - *Let (my) conversation be always full of grace, seasoned with salt, so that (I) may know how to answer everyone.*

Ephesians 4:32 NIV - *(Grant us gentle spirits so that we would) be kind and compassionate to one another, forgiving each other, just as in Christ God forgave you.*

1 Corinthians 12:24b-27 NIV - *But (you) God (have) put the body together, giving greater honor to the parts that lacked it, (and) so (I pray) that there (would) be no division in the body, but that its parts should have equal concern for each other. (Remind me that) If one part suffers, every part suffers with it; if one part is honored, every part rejoices with it.*

Hebrews 10:24-25 NIV - And let us consider how we may spur one another on toward love and good deeds, not giving up meeting together, as some are in the habit of doing, but encouraging one another - and all the more as you see the Day approaching.

I pray, Lord, that you would guide our words and actions as we strive to spur one another on toward love and good deeds. I pray that we would have hearts that long to meet together and encourage one another - all the more as we see the Day approaching.

Romans 12:10 ESV – Love one another with brotherly affection. Outdo one another in showing honor.
Give us humble hearts, Lord, so that we would honor one another above ourselves and so that we would be devoted to one another in love.

2 Corinthians 13:11 ESV – Finally, brothers, rejoice. Aim for restoration, comfort one another, agree with one another, live in peace; and the God of love and peace will be with you.
Unite us, Lord, as brothers and sisters. Guide us as we strive for full restoration. Give us words of encouragement for each other. I pray we would be of one mind and that we would live in peace. Thank you, Father, that you are the God of love and peace and that you will be with us every step of the way.

Colossians 3:13 NIV - *(Help us to) bear with each other and forgive one another if any of (us) has a grievance against someone. (Help us to) forgive as the Lord forgave (us).*

Matthew 6:14-15 ESV For if you forgive others their trespasses, your heavenly Father will also forgive you, but if you do not forgive others their trespasses, neither will your Father forgive your trespasses.
Grant me a forgiving heart, Lord, so I can fully forgive others for their trespasses against me.

Prayers for Times of Weariness

The Merriam-Webster dictionary defines weariness as "exhausted in strength, endurance, vigor, or freshness." Have you ever felt that way? Do you feel that way right now? God knows this world causes weariness and he has compassion for us. Throughout the Bible, God tells us He will be with us, he will refresh us, and he will give us rest during our times of weariness.

Matthew 11:28-29 ESV - "Come to me, all who labor and are heavy laden, and I will give you rest. Take my yoke upon you, and learn from me, for I am gentle and lowly in heart, and you will find rest for your souls."
Lord, I am weary and burdened. Thank you for an easy yoke. Grant me the rest I need.

Isaiah 40:29 NIV - He gives strength to the weary and increases the power of the weak.
Lord, I pray you would increase my power when I am weak and give me strength in my weariness.

Jeremiah 31:25 ESV – For I will satisfy the weary soul, and every languishing soul I will replenish.
Refresh my weary soul, Lord, and satisfy my spirit.

1 Peter 5:10 ESV - And after you have suffered a little while, the God of all grace, who has called you to his eternal glory in Christ, will himself restore, confirm, strengthen, and establish you.

Lord, I am suffering in my weariness. Thank you for the promise that you will restore me and make me strong, firm, and steadfast again. Help this truth to sink into my mind and heart so that it would bring me comfort.

Isaiah 40:31 NLT - But those who trust in the Lord will find new strength. They will soar high on wings like eagles. They will run and not grow weary. They will walk and not faint.
Father, help me to put my hope in you. I pray that that hope will renew my strength.

Psalm 3:3-5 NIV - *But you, Lord, are a shield around me, my glory, the one who lifts my head high. I call out to (you) Lord, and (you) answer me from (your) holy mountain. I lie down and sleep; I awake again, because (you) Lord sustain me.*

Colossians 3:1-2 NLT – Since you have been raised to new life with Christ, set your sights on the realities of heaven, where Christ sits in the place of honor at God's right hand. Think about the things of heaven, not the things of earth. For you died to this life, and your real life is hidden with Christ in God.
I confess that much of my weariness is because I have set my mind on earthly things. Help me, Lord, to set my heart on things above.

Habakkuk 3:17-18 NIV - *Though the fig tree does not bud and there are no grapes on the vines, though the olive crop fails and the fields produce no food, though there are no sheep in the pen and no cattle in the stalls, yet I will rejoice in (you) Lord, I will be joyful in God my Savior.*

Psalm 5:11 NIV - *But let all who take refuge in you be glad; let them ever sing for joy. Spread your protection over them, that those who love your name may rejoice in you.*

Galatians 6:9 NLT – So let's not get tired of doing what is good. At just the right time we will reap a harvest of blessing if we don't give up. *Thank you, Lord, for the hope of a harvest if I do not give up. May this motivate me to keep going and protect me from weariness.*

Prayers for Courage

God has a unique path for each of us, all for the purpose of His glory. Sometimes, the path he leads us down can be dark and ominous. We can easily become afraid and discouraged. For some, unfortunately, they decide the path forward is too difficult and they lose their faith altogether.

It doesn't need to come to that. God will always, always, always provide the courage and strength that we need to endure any and every obstacle we come across. Trust that He is always with you, even through the difficult seasons of your life. Do not throw away your confidence in Him, because that confidence in Him will be richly rewarded!

Hebrews 10:35-36 NLT – So do not throw away this confident trust in the Lord. Remember the great reward it brings you! Patient endurance is what you need now, so that you will continue to do God's will. Then you will receive all that he has promised.
Help me, Lord, to not throw away my confidence and, I pray, my confidence will be richly rewarded. Give me strength to persevere so that when I have done your will, I will receive what you have promised.

Joshua 1:9 NIV - Have I not commanded you? Be strong and courageous. Do not be afraid; do not be discouraged, for the Lord your God will be with you wherever you go.
Lord, you have commanded me to be strong and courageous, but I fail often in that regard. Protect me from fear and discouragement. I pray I would find encouragement in the fact that you are with me wherever I go.

2 Timothy 1:7 ESV – For God gave us a spirit not of fear but of power and love and self-control.

Thank you, Lord, for the spirit you have given me that does not make me timid, but gives me power, love, and self-control. I pray this truth would give me the courage I need to follow you wherever you lead me and to fulfill the plans you have for me.

Proverbs 1:33 ESV – but whoever listens to me will dwell secure and will be at ease, without dread of disaster.

Open my ears to hear you, Lord, so that I can listen to you, live in safety and be at ease, without fear of disaster.

1 Chronicles 28:20 NIV - David also said to Solomon his son, "Be strong and courageous, and do the work. Do not be afraid or discouraged, for the Lord God, my God, is with you. He will not fail you or forsake you until all the work for the service of the temple of the Lord is finished."

Thank you, Father, for guiding me through this plan you have for me and for being with me every step of the way. Give me strength and courage to do the work you would have me do, and protect me from the fear and discouragement that causes me to doubt the abilities you have given me.

Psalm 56:3-4 NIV - *When I am afraid, I put my trust in you. In God, whose word I praise - in God I trust and am not afraid. What can mere mortals do to me?*

1 Corinthians 16:13 NLT- Be on guard. Stand firm in the faith. Be courageous. Be strong.

Keep me alert, Lord, so I can be on my guard and stand firm in the faith. Give me courage and strength to continue, I pray.

Isaiah 41:10,13 NIV - So do not fear, for I am with you; do not be dismayed, for I am your God. I will strengthen you and help you; I will uphold you with my righteous right hand… For I am the Lord your God who takes hold of your right hand and says to you, Do not fear; I will help you.

Thank you, Lord, that I do not have to fear, because you are with me. Strengthen me, help me, and uphold me with your righteous right hand, I pray. You are the Lord my God, so I do not have to fear, because I know you will help me.

Psalm 27:14 NLT – Wait patiently for the Lord. Be brave and courageous. Yes, wait patiently for the Lord.

Give me the patience to wait on you, Lord. Help me to be strong, take heart, and wait for you. Thank you, that you are faithful to never leave me and to always guide me through the difficult valleys of my journey, with the sure hope of safe, green pastures ahead.

Ephesians 6:10 NIV - *Finally, (I pray I will) be strong in the Lord and in (your) mighty power.*

Prayers for Sin and Bondage

We are sinners. It's what comes naturally to us. But God calls us to be holy, as He is holy. Surely that is a very tall order, but God is faithful to help us.

Sometimes a sin takes root in our hearts so deeply, that we just can't seem to stop committing it. Maybe it's a certain behavior, or thought pattern, or even an addiction. We find ourselves in bondage to this sin and we can't seem to find our way out. There is a way out, though. The Word of God shows us how to break free from the sins that hold us in bondage, and God is faithful to never leave us as we struggle through these valleys.

Psalm 119:11 NLT - I have hidden your word in my heart that I might not sin against you.
Lord, I pray I can keep your word hidden in my heart and that your word would comfort me and keep me from sinning against you.

Hebrews 2:18 NIV - Because he himself suffered when he was tempted, he is able to help those who are being tempted.
Thank you, Lord, that you understand what I am going through. I pray for your help now to overcome this temptation.

2 Corinthians 7:1 NIV - Therefore, since we have these promises, dear friends, let us purify ourselves from everything that contaminates body and spirit, perfecting holiness out of reverence for God.
Since I have these promises from you, Lord, I want to purify myself from everything that contaminates my body and spirit. I want to perfect holiness out of reverence to you. But I feel weak, Lord. Give me strength to overcome this sin that has me in bondage. Help me to purge everything that contaminates my body and spirit.

Joshua 1:8 NLT – Study this Book of Instruction continually. Meditate on it day and night so you will be sure to obey everything written in it. Only then will you prosper and succeed in all you do.

I pray the Holy Spirit would help me to keep the Book of Instruction always on my lips and that the Spirit would help me to meditate on it day and night, so that I may be careful to do everything written in it.

2 Thessalonians 3:3 NLT - But the Lord is faithful; he will strengthen you and guard you from the evil one.

Lord, I pray you would strengthen me against the evil one who seeks to exploit my sin nature.

Hebrews 4:15-16 NIV - For we do not have a high priest who is unable to empathize with our weaknesses, but we have one who has been tempted in every way, just as we are - yet he did not sin. Let us then approach God's throne of grace with confidence, so that we may receive mercy and find grace to help us in our time of need.

You are the mighty God of creation. You did not need to subject yourself to the temptations that I face, but you did because of your love and mercy towards me. Because of your love and mercy I can confidently approach your throne of grace. Grant me grace and mercy in my time of need now, Lord. Empathize with my weakness and give me strength to overcome this temptation I am struggling with, I pray.

Romans 8:6 NIV - The mind governed by the flesh is death, but the mind governed by the Spirit is life and peace.

Lord, I confess my mind is governed by the flesh right now. Forgive me. I long for a mind governed by the Spirit. Show me the way to change the orientation of my mind. Have mercy on me and bring me to a place of peace.

James 4:7 NIV - Submit yourselves, then, to God. Resist the devil, and he will flee from you.

Lord, help me to see where I need to submit to you. Give me strength to resist the devil.

Galatians 6:8 NIV - Whoever sows to please their flesh will reap destruction; whoever sows to please the Spirit, from the Spirit will reap eternal life.

I confess I have sown to please my flesh and I have reaped destruction. Deliver me from my sin and show how to sow to please the Spirit, so that I will reap eternal life.

2 Corinthians 3:18 NIV - And we all, who with unveiled faces contemplate the Lord's glory, are being transformed into his image with ever-increasing glory, which comes from the Lord, who is the Spirit.

Like Moses, show me your glory, Lord, so I can contemplate you and be transformed into your image with ever-increasing glory, which comes from you.

1 John 1:8-9 NIV - If we claim to be without sin, we deceive ourselves and the truth is not in us. If we confess our sins, he is faithful and just and will forgive us our sins and purify us from all unrighteousness.

Lord, I confess my sin of _____. Thank you for your faithfulness to forgive me my sin and to purify me from all unrighteousness.

1 Corinthians 10:13 NIV - No temptation has overtaken you except what is common to mankind. And God is faithful; he will not let you be tempted beyond what you can bear. But when you are tempted, he will

also provide a way out so that you can endure it.

Lord, as I struggle with temptation, I pray your Spirit would constantly remind me that I am not facing a temptation I cannot bear. Make clear to me the way out that you are providing.

Prayers for Mourning

The death of a loved one is one of the most difficult experiences for us to process as Christians. We know that there is a glorious heaven above to enjoy with our Christian loved ones for eternity. But, what about right now? How can we possibly adjust to living a life without this person who was so close to us?

Even Jesus wept at the death of his friend, Lazarus. He knows what we are going through and he knows the pain that death causes those of us left behind. But, God is faithful. He is our comforter and he provides us with the rest that our grieving spirits need.

1 Peter 5:10 ESV – And after you have suffered a little while, the God of all grace, who has called you to his eternal glory in Christ, will himself restore, confirm, strengthen, and establish you.
Thank you, Father, for your loving kindness towards me in my time of mourning. Thank you that I can rest in your promise that you will restore, confirm, strengthen, and establish me.

Psalm 33:22 NIV - *May your unfailing love be with us, Lord, even as we put our hope in you.*

1 Corinthians 15:55-58 NIV - Where, O death, is your victory? Where, O death, is your sting? The sting of death is sin, and the power of sin is the law. But thanks be to God! He gives us victory through our Lord Jesus Christ. Therefore, my dear brothers and sisters, stand firm. Let nothing move you. Always give yourselves fully to the work of the Lord, because you know that your labor in the Lord is not in vain.

Thank you, Lord, for the salvation of my loved ones. Thank you that death is not the end, but that, through Jesus, we have victory over death. Help me to focus now on laboring for you and resting in the knowledge that death has no sting for those who believe in you.

1 Peter 1:3-6 NIV - Praise be to God and Father our Lord Jesus Christ! In his great mercy he has given us new birth into a living hope through the resurrection of Jesus Christ from the dead, and into an inheritance that can never perish, spoil or fade. This inheritance is kept in heaven for you, who through faith are shielded by God's power until the coming of the salvation that is ready to be revealed in the last time. In all this you greatly rejoice, though now for a little while you may have had to suffer grief in all kinds of trials.

Lord, as I am grieving now the loss of my loved one, I can rejoice in the new birth you have provided me. Thank you for an inheritance waiting for me in heaven. I pray you would comfort me now and that I can put my faith in you and your power until the coming of the salvation that is ready to be revealed.

Romans 5:3-5 NIV - Not only so, but we also glory in our sufferings, because we know that suffering produces perseverance; perseverance, character; and character, hope. And hope does not put us to shame, because God's love has been poured out into our hearts through the Holy Spirit, who has been given to us.

Lord, I am suffering now with this loss of my loved one. Help me to remember that this suffering is leading to perseverance, character, and hope.

John 11:35 ESV - Jesus wept.

Jesus wept at the death of his friend, as I weep now. Thank you, Lord, that you can sympathize with my suffering.

Psalm 34:18 ESV - The Lord is near to the brokenhearted and saves the crushed in spirit.

Thank you, Lord, for being close to me in my time of mourning. Thank you that you save those who are crushed in spirit.

Psalm 91:1-2 ESV – He who dwells in the shelter of the Most High will abide in the shadow of the Almighty. I will say to the Lord, "My refuge and my fortress, my God, in whom I trust."

Lord, you are my refuge and fortress in whom I trust. Provide me with rest from my grief as I dwell in your shelter.

Revelation 21:4 ESV – He will wipe every tear from their eyes, and death shall be no more, neither shall there be mourning, nor crying, nor pain anymore, for the former things have passed away.

Oh, Father, what a joyous day it will be when you wipe every tear from our eyes; when there is no more death or mourning, or pain! Help me, Lord, to put my hope in that future promise.

Prayers for Joy

"A saint doesn't know the joy of the Lord in spite of tribulation, but because of it." Oswald Chambers

All around us, we see a broken and desperate world. Strife and discord saturate the news and our Facebook feeds. No matter the circumstances around us, God makes his joy available to us. But, where is this joy and how do I find it? God's word shows us how to find his joy.

John 15:10-11 ESV - If you keep my commandments, you will abide in my love, just as I have kept my Father's commandments and abide in his love. These things I have spoken to you, that my joy may be in you and that your joy may be complete.
Help me, Lord, to keep your commandments and abide in your love so that your joy may be in me.

Romans 12:12 NIV - Be joyful in hope, patient in affliction, faithful in prayer.
Because of my hope in you, I can be joyful. Help me, Father, to be patient in affliction and faithful in prayer. May your joy overflow in my soul.

Matthew 2:9-10 NIV - After they had heard the king, they went on their way, and the star they had seen when it rose went ahead of them until it stopped over the place where the child was. When they saw the star, they were overjoyed.
Oh, Lord, I pray that I, like the wise men, would be overjoyed when I think of the birth of Jesus.

James 1:2-3 NIV - Consider it pure joy, my brothers and sister, whenever you face trials of many kinds, because you know that the testing of your faith produces perseverance. Let perseverance finish its work so that you may be mature and complete, not lacking anything.

I confess, I do not always consider it pure joy to suffer. Lord, forgive me and help me to remember that the trials I face will lead to perseverance and maturity. Grant me joy in the face of my trials.

Psalm 16:11 NIV - *You make known to me the path of life; you will fill me with joy in your presence, with eternal pleasures at your right hand.*

Psalm 30:5 NLT - For his anger lasts only a moment, but his favor lasts a lifetime! Weeping may last through the night, but joy comes in the morning.

Thank you that weeping does not last and that there is joy in the morning!

Proverbs 10:28 NIV - The prospect of the righteous is joy, but the hopes of the wicked come to nothing.

Lord, I pray you would help me to get rid of all wickedness in me. Show me the path to righteousness so that my prospect would be joy.

Hebrews 12:2b NIV - For the joy set before him he endured the cross, scorning its shame, and set down at the right hand of God.

Like Jesus, Lord, help me to focus on the joy set before me, so that I can face any trial that comes my way.

Psalm 51:12 NIV - *Restore to me the joy of your salvation and grant me a willing spirit, to sustain me.*

Isaiah 61:10 NLT - *I am overwhelmed with joy in the Lord my God! For he has dressed me with the clothing of salvation and draped me in a robe of righteousness. I am like a bridegroom dressed for his wedding or a bride with her jewels.*

Prayers for Finances

In these uncertain times, many of us worry about money. In very desperate times, we may even wonder where our next meal will come from. The Bible is full of reminders of God's graciousness towards us. He is our provider. The Bible is also filled with instructions on how we should view money/wealth and how we should use whatever we have to honor God. Praying through some of these Scriptures can reorient our perspectives towards money in a very powerful way.

Proverbs 11:28 NIV - Those who trust in their riches will fall, but the righteous will thrive like a green leaf.
Help me, Lord, to not put my faith, trust, and security into money, but to lead a life of righteousness so I might thrive like a green leaf.

Proverbs 11:24 - One person gives freely, yet gains even more; another withholds unduly, but comes to poverty.
Lord, I pray I would notice opportunities to give freely to others. Keep me from unduly withholding what you have given me.

Proverbs 11:24 NLT - Wealth is worthless in the day of wrath, but righteousness delivers from death.
Help me to see how worthless wealth is and lead me to righteousness instead, I pray.

Philippians 4:12-13 NIV - I know what it is to be in need, and I know what it is to have plenty. I have learned the secret of being content in any and every situation, whether well fed or hungry, whether living in plenty or in want. I can do all this through him who gives me strength.

Lord, I pray for contentment even now in my time of need. Help me to endure this time through You who gives me strength.

Proverbs 11:25 NLT - The generous person will prosper; those who refresh others will be themselves refreshed.
Lord, I pray for a spirit of giving, so that what I have would refresh others.

2 Corinthians 9:8 NLT - And God will generously provide all you need. Then you will always have everything you need and plenty left over to share with others.
Thank you, Lord, for providing all that I need with plenty left over. Help me to be a better steward of what you have provided.

Matthew 6:25-26 NLT - That is why I tell you not to worry about everyday life - whether you have enough food and drink, or enough clothes to wear. Isn't life more than food, and your body more than clothing? Look at the birds. They don't plant or harvest or store food in barns, for your heavenly Father feeds them. And aren't you more valuable to him than they are?
Thank you, Lord, that I am valuable to you. Forgive me for worrying about the necessities and forgetting that you are my provider. In your loving kindness, provide for mine and my family's immediate needs, I pray, and help me to trust that you will provide for us.

Habakkuk 3:17-18 NIV - *Though the fig tree does not bud and there are no grapes on the vines, though the olive crop fails and the fields produce no food, though there are no sheep in the pen and no cattle in the stalls, yet I will rejoice in the Lord, I will be joyful in God my Savior.*

1 Timothy 6:17 NIV - Command those who are rich in this present world not to be arrogant nor to put their hope in wealth, which is so uncertain, but to put their hope in God, who richly provides us with everything for our enjoyment.

Lord, I am guilty of placing my hope in wealth far too often. Forgive me and correct my thoughts. I pray my hope would be in you who richly provides us with everything for our enjoyment.

Proverbs 3:9 NIV - Honor the Lord with your wealth, with the firstfruits of your crops;

Too often I clench my fist around my money and hold tight. I pray, Lord, for a spirit that freely gives back to you what you have freely given to me. Help me to use whatever wealth I have to honor you.

Made in the USA
Monee, IL
02 April 2024

56215519R00048